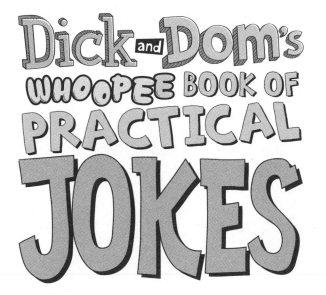

Dick and Dom's WHOOPEE BOOK OF PRACTICAL JOKES

Dick and Dom have reigned supreme for

many, many

years doing big fat and very silly stuff all over
your telly box!

The End.

PS: Many!

Also by Dick and Dom

Dick and Dom's Slightly Naughty but Very Silly Words

Dick and Dom's Big Fat and Very Silly Joke Book

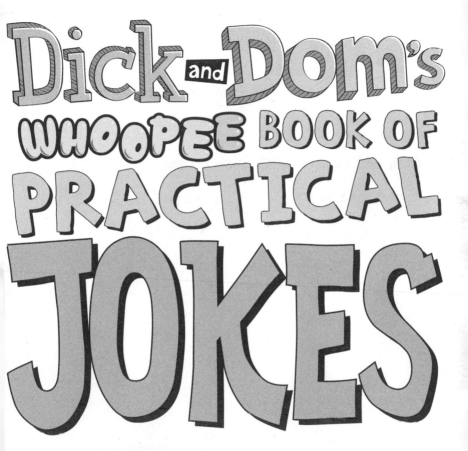

Dick and Dom's WHOOPEE BOOK OF PRACTICAL JOKES

INCLUDES TITTERS, NUGGETS AND MORE STUFF WHAT WE WROTE!

MACMILLAN CHILDREN'S BOOKS

FIRST PUBLISHED 2015 BY MACMILLAN CHILDREN'S BOOKS
AN IMPRINT OF PAN MACMILLAN
20 NEW WHARF ROAD, LONDON N1 9RR
ASSOCIATED COMPANIES THROUGHOUT THE WORLD
WWW.PANMACMILLAN.COM

ISBN 978-1-4472-8495-6

TEXT AND ILLUSTRATIONS COPYRIGHT © RICHARD McCOURT AND DARK WOOD PRODUCTIONS 2015
ILLUSTRATED BY DAVE CHAPMAN

THE RIGHT OF RICHARD McCOURT AND DARK WOOD PRODUCTIONS TO BE IDENTIFIED
AS THE AUTHORS OF THIS WORK HAS BEEN ASSERTED BY THEM IN
ACCORDANCE WITH THE COPYRIGHT, DESIGNS AND PATENTS ACT 1988.

3 5 7 9 8 6 4

A CIP CATALOGUE RECORD FOR THIS BOOK IS AVAILABLE FROM
THE BRITISH LIBRARY.

DESIGNED BY NIGEL HAZLE
PRINTED AND BOUND BY CPI GROUP (UK) LTD, CROYDON CR0 4YY

WE'VE ALREADY THANKED EVERYONE IN OUR
PAST TWO BOOKS SO . . . THIS BOOK IS
DEDICATED TO **YOU** . . . FAT FINGERS!

CONTENTS

INTRODUCTION 1
THE RULES OF PRACTICAL JOKING 2
BOUNCY PIDDLE 4
DEAD FINGER 6
CASH GRAB 10
LONG COTTON 12
SOME JOKES . . . INNIT 15
FLOATING BREAD ROLL 20
SAUSAGE FINGER 22
GLOW CHEEKS 26
LAY AN EGG 28
ED BANGER 30
BOGIES 34
PAPER RAIN 36
WET FEET 38
FIZZY-FROTHY-WHIZZY-BANG-BANG 40
STRIPY NOSE 42
THUMB PRICK 44
BOUNCY BOGIES 48
POPCORN SURPRISE 52
YOU'VE WON! 54
STUCK COIN 56
SCHOOL JOKES 59
APPLE WORM 64
BOG-ROLL SHOE 66
MULTICOLOURED CEREAL 68
ZOO CALL 72
SUGAR 'N' SALT SWAP 74
STICKY BIRO 76
FISH FINGERS 78
FROTHY COFFEE 82
WATERY BONCE 84
STICKY SWITCH 86

RUBBISH EGGS	90
SUCKER	92
SMILE, DAVE - YOU'RE ON THE TOILET	95
DICK AND DOM'S SLIGHTLY-NAUGHTY-BUT-VERY- SILLY WORDSEARCH	96
ARM RISER	98
LOOP THE LOOP	102
FROZEN PUFFS	104
UN-HAPPY BIRTHDAY	106
MORE RANDOM JOKES	108
BLACK-EYE TELESCOPE	112
THE LONG WAIT	116
DRINKING CHALLENGE	118
GHOST AT THE WINDOW	120
BANSHEE SHRIEK	121
WHOOOOOOO WAIL	122
BAD MOUSE	123
PHANTOM SPECIAL EFFECTS	124
DAVE THE DUMMY	126
JELLY JUICE	128
ANSWER PHONEY	130
MONSTER JOKES	132
WAKEY WAKEY!	134
HEAVY BAG	138
CRAZY, CRAZY KITCHEN CUPBOARDS	141
BOG BUBBLES	142
MINTY BICCY	143
BEACH BUM	144
FOAM FACE	145
THE INCREDIBLE SHRINKING CLOTHES	146
STRING OF PANTS	148
BALLOONY	151
WALLPAPER SWITCHY-SWATCH	152
DON'T BE LATE!	154
CEREAL MIX-UP	156

CEREAL NUTS	158
KONNICHIWA	162
DIN-DIN MIX-UP	164
FACE PLANT	166
HOMEMADE ITCHING POWDER	168
BANANA-RAMA	174
DIY FAKE DOGGY DOO	176
ANIMAL JOKES	179
SNOT HEAD	183
TOFFEE ONION	184
DOUGHNUT SURPRISE	186
HAPPY CLEANING	188
DO AS YOU'RE TOLD!	190
EVEN MORE RANDOM JOKES	191
STUCK!	196
SQUASHED FLY	198
FLOATING LUMP	199
CLEAN YOUR GLASSES	201
LUMPY TUMMY	202
PLOP ON THE SEAT	205
BANANA-SKIN SURPRISE	206
CLOWN TIME!	207
DICK AND DOM'S BIG FAT CROSSWORD	210
MUSIC JOKES	212
SPIDER HIDER	214
JELLY WORMS	215
LOTTO WIN-WIN!	216
SUPERSIZE SHOP	218
TIC-TAC TEETH	220
BIG-CAR SURPRISE	222
FOOTBALL JOKES	223
SPECIAL DELIVERY	227
REAL 'SPONGE' CAKE	228
FAKEY FLIES	230
CATCHING NOTHING	231
ANSWERS	232

Introduction

Can you imagine how much fun it was to write a practical-joke book?

Well, it wasn't! For two months we sat in a tiny box at the side of a motorway surrounded by the bosses of the book company who were wearing grass skirts and holding spears.

Every time we thought we'd finished, they'd just shout out 'Bad Bongos!' and poke us.

In the end, we finally finished it and what lies before you is something that will change your life,* will change the world** and will change your bed sheets.***

*No it won't.
**It really won't.
***Possibly?

The Rules of Practical Joking

Now listen here, fat heads! When doing a practical joke, please be mindful of *where* you do them, to *whom* you do them and *when* you do them.

For example, don't throw a water bomb at your ninety-eight-year-old grandma, especially if she has the squits. And don't do the fake dog-poo thing on your trip to Buckingham Palace . . . You get the idea!

WARNING!

Some of these jokes require using sharp things such as scissors, cooking things in the oven or on the hob, or using superglue. Remember that you must **ALWAYS** get an adult to help you **(NO EXCUSES! DO IT!)** when using scissors or knives, cooking *or* using super-sticky superglue.

You'll know if a practical joke means using any of these things when you see this symbol:

This way you'll be able to pull off amazing practical jokes without getting any burny burns, hurty cuts or accidentally gluing your shoes to your face!

ABOVE ALL . . .

Prat about responsibly! Don't EVER play a practical joke on someone if you think it will upset them. Upsetting people on purpose is never funny and, if you think it is, it ISN'T . . . OK? I mean what kind of monster are you? People like you make us sick! Now go to your bedroom and cry while playing the trombone.

Don't EVER try practical jokes that could hurt anyone!

And remember YOU may well be pranked back. If you are . . . laugh! Laugh hard! In fact, laugh so hard that you fart out of your mouth!

Bouncy Piddle

Help Dave* to have an
extremely memorable
trip to the bog.**

You need:
Clingfilm
A toilet
Dave

How to do it:
Lift up the toilet seat.

Cover your toilet bowl with cling film and
put the seat back down.

Wait for Dave to go for a wee and wait for
the screams as his piddle bounces all
over the bathroom!

*We *always* use Dave for our practical jokes. You can use one of your own mates, *or* Dave. If he's not too busy!

This is Dave.

Look at him . . . He's an idiot! Dave is the kind of dribbly twit that falls for *any* practical joke. He's the kind of guy that walks into a wall while looking at the wall and saying, 'Wow, look, a wall . . . I really hope I don't walk into that wall.'

Every practical joke in this book has been tried and tested on Dave,*** proving that the contents of this book are better than pig fat on toast!

**You may a need a mop!

***It hasn't. We made that up, because we're anarchists!

Dead Finger

Make Dave scream as you show him your chopped-off moving finger in a matchbox!

You need:
A small empty matchbox
Scissors
Cotton wool
Ketchup (or something red –
not actual blood!)
Talcum powder
Dave

How to do it:
Remove the inside tray
of the matchbox and
cut a finger-sized hole
towards one end using the
scissors.

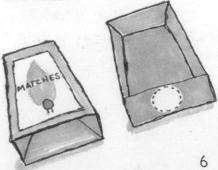

Shove your finger through the hole so it sits inside the tray. Then surround your finger with cotton wool and talcum powder it so it looks dead.

Squeeze a bit of ketchup round the bottom of your finger, then slide the matchbox cover back over the tray. Bosh! You now have a dead finger in a matchbox.

Show Dave your finger by sliding the lid of the matchbox back. When he goes to touch the dead finger, wiggle it and hear Dave scream!

Dick's Wise Monkey Says . . .

When confused, take
a moment to walk outside,
look at the sky, breathe deeply,
channel your energy . . .
and let one rip.

THE DAILY BUM

First Edition   Monday 5th June

World - Business - Finance - Lifestyle - Travel - Sport - Weather

Bruce Forsyth's Ears Turn into Batteries

Blah blah blah blah blah blah blah blah blah blah blah blah blah blah blah blah blah blah blah blah blah blah blah blah blah blah blah blah blah blah blah blah blah blah blah blah blah blah blah blah

Farmer Milks Wasp

Blah blah blah blah blah blah blah blah blah blah blah blah blah blah blah blah blah blah blah blah blah blah blah blah blah blah blah blah blah blah blah blah blah blah blah blah blah blah blah blah

Man Gets Trapped in Pencil

Blah blah

9

Ooooh!

Cash Grab

Confuse someone's brain when they think
they've found a fiver but it keeps flying off!

> *You need:*
> A fiver
> Fishing wire
> Sticky tape
> Dave

How to do it:
Use sticky tape to stick the
end of the fishing wire to the
fiver. Put the fiver on the floor,
then hide round the corner (but
make sure you can still see the
money).

When Dave appears and tries to pick up the fiver, tug on the fishing wire to pull it out of his grasp.

Repeat this until he sees you, then shout 'Mandy Dingle!' and leg it.

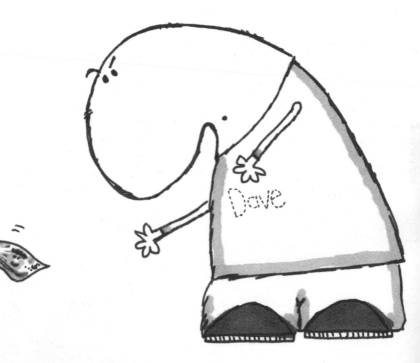

Long Cotton

When Dave tries to pick a piece of loose cotton off your clothes, he ends up pulling out loads . . . and loads . . . and loads of cotton.

You need:
Cotton reel
Needle
Jacket with an
    inside pocket
Dave

How to do it:
Thread the needle with the cotton. Push the needled cotton from the inside of your jacket to the outside.

Remove the needle, leaving about two centimetres of dangly cotton and place the rest of the reel in your inside jacket pocket.

Ask Dave to remove the piece of dangly cotton and he will keep pulling out loads and loads and loads of cotton . . . and more cotton . . . and more cotton . . .
until he pulls out
Fearne Cotton!

Fearne →

Dick and Dom's **TOP FIVE** Things to Eat with Chips

1) Chips and chips and chips

2) Lemon pips and chips

3) Asparagus tips and chips

4) Llamas' lips and chips

5) Mr Tumble's hips and chips

Some Jokes . . . Innit

Written by Barry the Chimp, who likes dressing up as a girl and throwing his bum product at the wall while swinging from a chandelier

What has four legs, a tail, and flies?
A dead horse.

What do you get if you cross the Atlantic with the *Titanic*?
Halfway.

Where did Napoleon keep his armies?
Up his sleevies.

What was Nelson's little brother called?
Half Nelson.

I AM HALF NELSON. (WHICH IS ALSO A HOLD IN WRESTLING) ... SO, THIS IS A GOOD JOKE IF YOU ARE A FAN OF WRESTLING OR 18th-CENTURY VICE-ADMIRALS.

What's invisible and smells like carrots?
Bunny farts.

DOM: What would it take for you to kiss me?
DICK: Anaesthetic.

Why did the pilot land his plane on top of the house?
Because the landing lights were on.

I'm not saying I find you annoying, but you could give a headache to an aspirin.

Waiter, do you have frogs' legs?
No, sir, it's just the way I walk.

DOM: Did you miss me while I was away?
DICK: Have you been away?

How does an Irish potato
change its nationality?
When it becomes a French fry.

My dad was a Pole.
North or South?

Floating Bread Roll

A bread roll floats about like you have some kind of wizardy, freaky ways. (Well, what did you think was going to happen?)

You need:
Bread roll
Fork
Tea towel
Dave

How to do it:
Stick the bread roll on the end of the fork. Then hold the tea towel by the two top corners so that it hangs down square in front of you.

At the same time, keep hold of the handle of the fork in your right hand so the fork and bread roll are secretly hidden behind the tea towel.

Keeping the tea towel square, lift the fork handle up so that just the bread roll pops up above the top edge of the tea towel. Then move it down and push it into the middle of the tea towel.

Dave will think it is a bready-tea-towel-ghosty thingy!

Sausage Finger

Dave will be in bits when he realizes that one of your fingers is a sausage!

You need:
A cooked sausage
Dave

How to do it:
Ask a grown-up to help you cook a sausage and let it cool.

Put the cooled sausage between two of your fingers so it looks as though you've got five fingers and a thumb on one hand.

Ask Dave to shake your
hand and then pull away
and leave him holding a
sausage finger!

Squirt some brown sauce all
over it and tell him to shove it
in his gob.

Blanky, Blanky, Blanky!

Fill in the blanks to make up your own stories.

Once there was a _____ woman

who had a wonky _____. She

visited Doctor _____ who

said, 'You've got a problem with your

_____.' The doctor took out a

screwdriver.

WOW!

He removed her_____ and

reattached it to her _____.

'All done!' said the doctor.

The woman got up and replied,

'_____, I feel absolutely

_____ now. Thanks, Doc, you

really are an utter _____.'

Glow Cheeks

Your cheeks will glow as if they are a pair of chubby, illuminated overweight fireflies.

You need:
Torch
A dark room
Dave

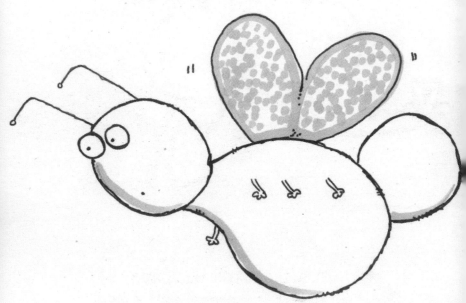

How to do it:
Go into a dark room
with Dave.

Shove the torch in your
mouth and puff out your
cheeks.

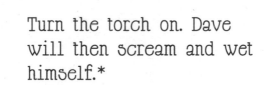

Turn the torch on. Dave
will then scream and wet
himself.*

*Possibly. You may need a mop.

Lay an Egg

Dave will think you've gone clucking mad as he watches you pop out an egg!

You need:
An egg
Dave

Er...

How to do it:
Crouch down on the floor and shout out, 'Hey, Dave, I'm going to lay one!'

As you crouch down, secretly place an egg (either hard-boiled or plastic) between your squished-together legs.

Shake your head and make your face go purple as if you are having a dumpasaurus.* Scream like a chicken, flap your arms, then stand back up.

As you stand back up, the egg will be released and Dave will do a vom goblin!*

*See *Slighty Naughty but Very Silly Words.*

Ed Banger

Dave will think that you are whacking your head really hard against a door while saying your ABCs!

You need:
A door
Dave

How to do it:
Tell Dave you've learned a brilliant way to get your ABCs into your head, and that you're going to recite them to him.

Make sure Dave is standing behind you. With the door closed, start saying your ABCs and, for every letter you

say, pretend to bang your head on the door while secretly kicking your foot loudly against the bottom of the door.

NB: Do not actually hit your head against the door, as this will cause massive bruising and be all hurty.

Dick's Wise Monkey Says . . .

As the wise monk
Jim Hi Wan once said to
me . . . 'Can I borrow
your iPhone 6 charger?'

THE DAILY BUM

First Edition   Monday 5th June

World - Business - Finance - Lifestyle - Travel - Sport - Weather

Andy Murray Uses Goose as Racket

Blah blah blah blah blah blah blah blah blah blah blah blah blah blah blah blah blah blah blah blah blah blah blah blah blah blah blah blah blah blah blah blah blah blah blah blah blah blah blah blah blah blah blah blah blah blah blah blah blah blah blah blah blah blah blah blah blah blah blah blah blah blah blah blah blah blah blah blah blah blah blah blah

Tess Daly Made of Clay

Blah blah blah blah blah blah blah blah blah blah blah blah blah blah blah blah blah blah blah blah blah blah blah blah blah blah blah blah blah blah blah blah blah blah blah blah blah blah blah blah blah blah blah blah blah blah blah blah blah

Man Marries Broom

Blah blah

Bogies

Dave will not understand how so much snot can come from your fat conk!

You need:
White linen handkerchief
Green washing-up
   liquid
Dave

Gosh!

How to do it:
In secret, lay the handkerchief over the palm of your hand. Squeeze an egg cup's worth of washing-up liquid into the middle and close your hand into a fist, hiding the pretend bogies.

WOW!

Find Dave and tell him you're not feeling well and you've got snot. Then do the biggest pretend sneeze on to your closed hanky fist. Open your hand up to reveal . . . BOGIES!

Paper Rain

Make an umbrella that keeps off
the drizzle, but covers Dave in paper .

You need:
An old newspaper
An umbrella
Dave

How to do it:
In secret, rip up
the newspaper
into billions of
tiny little pieces.
Open the umbrella
and put it on the
floor, then shove
the ripped-up paper
into the inside of
the umbrella and
close it.

Ooooh!

Wait until it's raining, then kindly offer to lend Dave your umbrella. When he opens the brolly, he'll get covered in paper rain.

Wet Feet

Dave will get wet feet like a gecko!

I'm an irrelevant gecko!

You need:
A plastic water bottle
  with screw top
Scissors
Dave

How to do it:

Make small holes in the bottom of the water bottle (careful with the scissors).

Fill the bottle with water and screw the lid on tightly. Science will stop the water leaking through the holes.

Find Dave and ask him to unscrew the bottle. When he does, the water will leak out through the holes and Dave will get wet feet.

Fizzy-Frothy-Whizzy-Bang-Bang

Watch Dave's glass of Coke go more nuts than a packet of . . . NUTS!

You need:
An ice-cube tray
Mentos
Water
Glass of Diet Coke
Dave

How to do it:
In secret, put a Mentos in each section of an ice-cube tray, then fill the tray with water and send it to the Arctic to freeze.*

Once the ice has set, find Dave and offer him a lovely fizzy drink.

Pour Dave his glass of Diet Coke,
pop in the Mentos ice cubes and
after about a minute the ice cubes
will melt and it will all go fizzy-
frothy-whizzy-bang-bang!

*Or use a freezer.

Stripy Nose

Dave will think he's playing a fun game with a coin, but ends up with lead on his hooter.

You need:
Piece of paper
Pencil
2p coin
Dave

How to do it:
Tell Dave you are making some targets, then draw a circle round the coin on the paper several times in different places.

Tell Dave the rules: he has to get the coin to land on a target by rolling the coin down his nose.

Dave will think he's playing a brilliant game, but actually the pencil lead will rub off on to his nose giving him a stripy schnozz!

Thumb Prick

Dave will put a needle in your thumb, but it won't hurt! He's such an idiot.

You need:
The end of a carrot the same
   size as your thumb
Handkerchief
Needle
Dave

How to do it:

Hide the carrot in your hand and stick your thumb up in the air. Cover your thumb with the handkerchief and secretly switch your thumb for the carrot.

Ask Dave to stick a needle in it and it won't hurt! (Dave will be *really* impressed.)

NB: Make sure that you remember to switch your thumb for the carrot, or you'll really get a needle in your thumb!

Dick and Dom's **TOP FIVE** Things to Swim In

1) Cockles

2) Goose fat

3) Pesto pasta

4) Squits

5) Mandurah Manga Kalan (look it up!)

THE DAILY BUM

First Edition   Monday 5th June

World - Business - Finance - Lifestyle - Travel - Sport - Weather

Family Moves into Breadbin

Blah blah blah blah blah blah blah blah blah blah blah blah blah blah blah blah blah blah blah blah blah blah blah blah blah blah blah blah blah blah blah blah blah blah blah blah blah blah blah blah blah blah blah blah blah blah blah blah blah blah blah blah blah blah blah blah blah blah blah blah blah blah blah blah blah blah blah blah blah blah blah blah blah blah blah blah blah blah blah blah blah

GOAT VOTED SWEDISH PRIME MINSTER

Blah blah blah blah blah blah blah blah blah blah blah blah blah blah blah blah blah blah blah blah blah blah blah blah blah blah blah blah blah blah blah blah blah blah blah blah blah blah blah blah blah blah blah blah blah blah blah blah

Rooney First Footballer in Space

Blah blah

Bouncy Bogies

When you sneeze into your handkerchief, your bogies will bounce around the room!

> **You need:**
> A bouncy ball
> Handkerchief
> Needle and thread
> Dave

How to do it:
In secret, put the ball into the handkerchief and fold it in half. Sew the handkerchief together so the ball is hidden inside.

Next time you see Dave, pretend to sneeze into your handkerchief and then throw it on the floor.

It will then amaze Dave by bouncing back up to you!

Blanky, Blanky, Blanky!

Fill in the blanks to make up your own stories.

A man went to the shops and bought a tiny

little _____. Whenever he poked

it, it made a _____ noise. He took

it to the _____ and then, instead

of it making the _____ noise, it

made a loud _____!

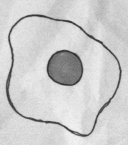

'This is terrible!' said the man, so he took

it back to the shops and changed it for

a _____, which he cooked

and ate with _____ and

_____.

Popcorn Surprise

Scare the hell out of Dave when a hand shoots out of a bucket of popcorn.

You need:
Bucket of popcorn
Scissors
Dave

Ooooh!

How to do it:
Before you sit down
to watch a movie
with Dave, empty
the popcorn into
a bowl and
use scissors
to cut a hole
in the
bottom
of the
popcorn
bucket.

Put your hand through the hole, then pour the popcorn back into bucket.

When you sit next to Dave to watch the movie, offer the twit some popcorn.

When he goes for a piece, quickly grab his hand and laugh at the panic on his fat wet face!

You've Won!

Confuse Dave on the phone.

You need:
A phone
Dave

How to do it:
Call Dave.

When he answers, simply say:
'You've won!'

When he says: 'Won what?'
You reply: 'You've won!'

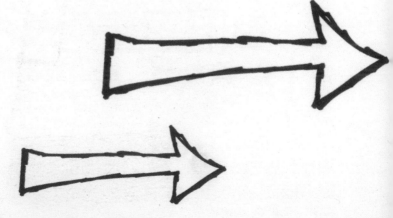

From now, whatever he asks, simply say: 'You've won!'

When Dave finally gets really angry and yells, 'WHAT HAVE I WON?', leave a long pause. Then say, 'Nothing,' and put down the phone.

Stuck Coin

Watch Dave trying to pick up a £1 coin from the pavement but failing badly.

You need:
£1 coin
Superglue
Dave

How to do it:
       Squeeze some superglue on to the coin and stick it to a pavement.

Find Dave and suggest you go for a walk. When you both see the money on the pavement, turn to Dave, smile and whisper, 'Pick up that pound because I need to buy a new shower cap.' When Dave tries to pick up the money, he can't.

Start shouting,
'Pick up that
pound coin
as I need to
buy a FLIPPIN'
shower cap! PICK UP THAT POUND COIN
AS I NEED TO BUY A FLIIIIIIPPIIIN'
SHHHOOOOWEERRRR CAAAAAAAAAP!'

Keep shouting this
until Dave's head
pops off (and
he won't need a
shower cap)!

School Jokes

Written by Mr Smithy – the musty, tank-top-loving, bad-breathed, boss-eyed, short-legged, baldy-slap-head science teacher from Frapton

TEACHER: What nationality are you?
NEW KID: Well, my father was born in Iceland and my mother was born in Cuba. So I reckon that makes me an ice cube.

What did the constipated maths teacher do?
Worked it out with a pencil.

Our teacher's an ancient treasure.
We often wonder who dug her up . . .

TEACHER: Dick, can you
find New Zealand on
the map, please?
DICK: There it is, sir.
TEACHER: Now, Dom, who
discovered New Zealand?
DOM: Dick did.

TEACHER: What do we do
with crude oil?
*DOM: Teach it some
manners.*

TEACHER: If I had 15 marbles in my right trouser pocket, 25 marbles in my left trouser pocket, 20 marbles in my right hip pocket and 30 marbles in my left hip pocket – what would I have?

DICK: *Heavy trousers, sir.*

TEACHER: Are you going to visit Egypt?

DICK: *I sphinx so.*

TEACHER: You missed school yesterday, didn't you, Dom?

DOM: *Not even slightly.*

TEACHER: What can you tell me about Queen Victoria?
DICK: She's dead.

TEACHER: The human brain is a wonderful thing. It's a pity yours came from a monkey.

DICK: I think my English teacher loves me.
DOM: Why?
DICK: She keeps putting little kisses all over my homework just like these: X X X X!

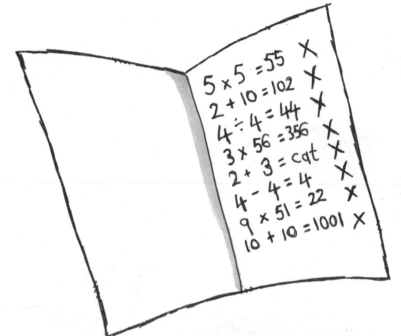

Teacher! Teacher! I don't want to go to France.
Shut up and keep swimming!

Apple Worm

Dave finds a little friend in his mid-morning snack.

You need:
A Granny Smith apple
Two gummy worms
A spoon
Dave

How to do it:

Hollow out a couple of small holes in the side of the apple – you don't need to use a knife for this; a spoon will do – and shove in the gummy worms as far as they'll go.

Give Dave his treat and watch him squirm with delight as he comes face to face with the wiggly worms.

Bog-Roll Shoe

Dave will think his shoes
have shrunk.

You need:
Toilet roll
Dave's shoes
Dave

How to do it:
When Dave isn't looking,
nick his shoes and stuff
loads of toilet roll into
the front of them.

Invite Dave to go for a walk
and when he accepts watch him
try to squeeze his massive feet
into his already packed blue
suede shoes.

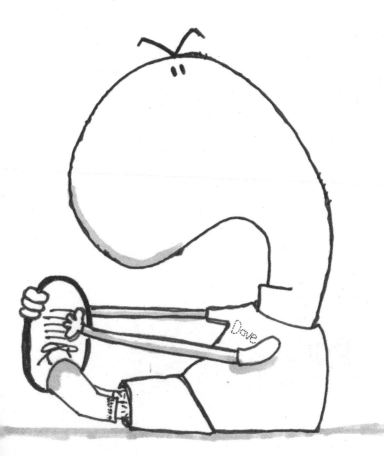

Multicoloured Cereal

Dave will think there is something seriously wrong with his breakfast.

You need:
Dave's bowl of cornflakes
  (or any other cereal)
Food colouring
Milk
Dave

Food
Colouring

Like hairdye for
food. Except you
can eat it.

How to do it:

Before Dave comes down for breakfast, get his cereal ready by pouring a few drops of the food colouring into his empty breakfast bowl.

Pour the cornflakes on top to hide the food colouring.

When Dave pours the milk on to his cornflakes, it will start changing colour.

Ooooh

Dick and Dom's **TOP FIVE** Things to Use Your Nan for

1) Garlic nan

2) Peshwari nan

3) Plain nan

4) Keema nan

5) A diving board

Zoo Call

Trick Dave into thinking he's a sea-lion lover.

You need:
A phone
The number for your local zoo
A piece of paper
A pencil
Dave

How to do it:
Write down on a piece of paper that Dave needs to return a phone call.

Include the number of the local zoo (but don't tell him who it is), and tell him that he needs to ask to speak to Mr C. Lion.

A call? for Me How super

Laugh hysterically when the zoo accuses
Dave of playing a joke on *them*.

Throw a fish at Dave.

Sugar 'n' Salt Swap

Ever wondered what the salty tea tastes like?
Dave has.

You need:
A sugar bowl
A salt dispenser or pot
Dave

Not really sugar... obvs.

How to do it:
Empty the sugar bowl and fill
it with salt. At the same time
empty the salt pot and fill it
with sugar.

Sugar disguised as Salt

Salt disguised as Sugar

You don't have to do
anything straight away
just . . . just let it happen.

You'll be able to tell from Dave's face when it does!

NB: Remember not to have any sugar on your cereal until you've switched the sugar and the salt back.

Sticky Biro

Watch strong old Dave become a weak ninny as he struggles to remove the top from a pen.

You need:
A pen
Paper
Superglue
Dave

How to do it:
Get your grown-up to superglue the pen lid to the pen.

CAUTION

Find Dave and make a bet with him that he can't write his name in 15 seconds. Give him the pen and start the clock.

Dave will grunt, squeak, groan and potentially trump as he finds that he can't get the lid off the pen, and he loses the bet!

Fish Fingers

Dave will get fishy fingers!

You need:
Fish paste
A doorknob
Dave

How to do it:
Smear fish paste on Dave's
doorknob when he's out.

When Dave gets home, he will go to
open the door and his hand will get
covered in fish paste.

THE DAILY BUM

First Edition   Monday 9th June

World - Business - Finance - Lifestyle - Travel - Sport - Weather

IPHONE 17S WILL HAVE BUILT-IN TOASTER

Blah blah blah blah blah blah blah blah blah blah blah blah blah blah blah blah blah blah blah blah blah blah blah blah blah blah blah blah blah blah blah blah blah blah blah blah blah blah blah blah blah blah blah blah blah blah blah blah blah blah blah blah

Granny Eaten After Inventing Real-life 'Hungry Hippos'

Blah blah blah blah blah blah blah blah blah blah blah blah blah blah blah blah blah blah blah blah blah blah blah blah blah blah blah blah blah blah blah blah blah blah blah blah blah blah blah blah blah blah blah blah blah blah blah blah

Royal Family Turned Away from Gulliver's Kingdom for Not Having Correct Change

Blah blah blah blah blah blah blah blah blah blah blah blah blah blah blah blah blah blah blah blah blah blah blah blah blah blah blah blah blah blah blah blah blah blah blah blah blah blah blah blah blah blah blah blah blah blah blah blah blah blah blah blah blah blah blah blah blah blah blah blah blah blah blah blah blah blah blah blah blah blah blah blah blah blah blah blah blah blah blah blah blah blah blah blah blah blah blah blah blah blah blah blah

Ooooh!

Dick's Wise Monkey Says...

Never let the things you *want* make you forget the things you *have* – unless you *have* everything you *want*, so you never forget the things you *have* – because you *have* everything and never forget anything you *have*.

Frothy Coffee

Watch Dave's mocha-frappé-whoppa-floppaccino froth over.

> *You need:*
> A sugar bowl
> Baking powder
> A kettle and some coffee or tea
> Dave

How to do it:
Replace the sugar in the sugar bowl with some baking powder, then disguise what you've done by covering the baking powder with a little sugar on top.

HOLLYWOOD VERSION OF THIS PRACTICAL JOKE

Offer Dave a delicious hot beverage. When Dave puts some of the 'sugar' in his coffee or tea, he will be in for a shock as his mocha-frappé-whoppa-floppaccino will start foaming.

Watery Bonce

Dave will get a wet head.

You need:
A plastic cup full of water
A door that opens 'into'
    a bathroom
Dave

How to do it:
Open the door just wide
enough so that Dave can
walk straight in without
touching the door, then
balance the plastic cup
full of water on the top
of the door.

Ooooh!

When Dave needs a piddle, he will walk into the bathroom and try to close the door. This will make the cup come flying down, which will give Dave a wet head.

Sticky Switch

Dave won't be able to turn the light on.

You need:
Sticky tape
A light switch
Dave

How to do it:
Stick a piece of tape over a light switch, making sure you cover the whole thing so that the switch doesn't move when you press it.

Ask Dave to turn on the light for you. When he tries to press it, it won't work.

I can't... My fingers don't seem to work.

Blanky, Blanky, Blanky!

Fill in the blanks to make up your own stories.

Dick and Dom went to the _____

and bumped into _____, who

was carrying a wet, soggy and slightly

muddy _____.

'Where did you get that?' asked Dick.

Gosh!

'I found it down the back of my

_____,' said _____.

'What are you going to do with it?' said Dom.

'I'm going to find the nearest pig and

put it on its _____,' said

_____ cheerfully.

Rubbish Eggs

Dave won't be able to make his eggy
breakfast.

You need:
A box of eggs
Dave

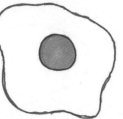

How to do it:
With the help of your
grown-up, boil all six
eggs until they are hard –
but make sure Dave doesn't
see you doing this!

Let the eggs cool down and then put them
back in the egg box.

When Dave goes to make his eggy brekkie, he won't be able to crack the eggs.

Spot the odd egg out for an 'eggciting' bonus prize of nothing!

Sucker

Dave won't be able to slurp up his lovely drink. Poor Dave!

You need:
A straw
A pin or toothpick
A drink
Dave

How to do it:
Secretly make one or two small holes in a drinking straw above the level of where the drink comes to. You could use a toothpick to make the holes, or a pin.

Offer to make Dave a nice drink with the straw in it.

Watch Dave as he struggles to slurp up the drink through the holey straw!

Dick and Dom's **TOP FIVE** Homework Excuses

1) My dog ate it

2) My dog sat on it

3) My dog wrote it

4) My dog's pregnant

5) My dog's dead

Smile, Dave – You're on the Toilet

Dave will have a surprising experience next time he goes to the toilet.

You need:
A toilet roll
A pen
Dave

How to do it:
Unroll a strip of
toilet paper. About
four or five sheets
along from the end
write: 'Smile! You're
on CCTV!'

Roll up the toilet
roll to how it was
before and put it back on the
toilet-roll holder.

Next time Dave goes to drop his guts, he'll
see your note and get very worried.

Dick and Dom's Slightly-Naughty-but-Very-Silly Wordsearch

C	B	R	E	B	Z	F	U	T	T	O	C	S	O	U
O	T	O	L	O	N	G	B	O	N	G	O	S	L	M
B	R	K	R	E	F	T	E	E	Q	G	B	T	F	B
B	G	E	R	M	R	A	I	N	U	L	G	R	W	O
L	N	E	Q	U	I	B	S	N	O	O	S	E	A	B
E	K	F	E	R	V	E	P	O	N	P	Z	H	T	O
R	R	T	W	A	G	G	L	E	B	O	R	K	S	L
W	I	Y	A	K	Y	A	K	T	R	U	M	P	E	T
O	W	C	P	B	E	H	P	S	G	L	A	F	D	P
B	O	R	L	S	A	H	A	R	A	H	O	O	T	A
B	T	U	I	W	E	S	F	I	Q	U	E	W	T	V
L	D	D	P	S	X	V	O	M	G	O	B	L	I	N
E	A	D	E	R	H	Y	E	B	H	J	B	E	F	L
R	T	L	I	T	T	L	E	N	O	E	L	L	Y	Y
E	W	E	R	Q	B	U	M	A	L	A	R	M	T	M
O	S	W	A	L	D	C	H	O	P	S	G	I	F	U

See page 232 for answers

GERM RAIN

KREFT

OSWALDCHOPS

FUTTOCS

SAHARAHOOTA

PLIP

VOM GOBLIN

WOT DAT

UMBOBO

COBBLER WOBBLER

LITTLE NOELLY

FWATS

YAK YAK TRUMPET

BUM ALARM

QUON

CRUDDLE

LONG BONGOS

TWAGGLEBORKS

See *Dick and Dom's Slightly Naughty but Very Silly Words* to find out what these words mean!

Arm Riser

Dave's arm will rise up on its own. Spooky!

You need:
A wall
Dave's arm

How to do it:
Ask Dave to press his arm
against the wall (not too hard)
and count to ten.

WOW!

When Dave moves his arm away from the wall, the pressure will make it rise up all on its own!

THE DAILY BUM

First Edition • Monday 5th June

World - Business - Finance - Lifestyle - Travel - Sport - Weather

David Cameron Gives Birth to a Cheesecake

Blah blah blah blah blah blah blah blah blah blah blah blah blah blah blah blah blah blah blah blah blah blah blah blah blah blah blah blah blah blah blah blah blah blah blah blah blah blah blah blah blah blah blah blah blah blah blah blah blah blah blah blah blah blah blah blah blah blah blah blah blah blah blah blah blah blah blah blah blah blah blah blah blah blah blah blah blah blah blah blah blah blah blah blah blah blah blah blah blah blah

MP'S WIFE CAUGHT IN THE NORTH SEA

Mr Tumble's Waistcoat Made of Tarmac

Blah blah

Ooool

Dick's Wise Monkey Says . . .

There are some things money can't buy . . . like manners, morals, intelligence or that big-time remote-control pig from Toys R Us . . . It's well expensive and sick!

Loop the Loop

Dave will be driven loop-the-loopy by this silly trick!

You need:
Your voice
Dave

How to do it:
Whatever question Dave asks you, give him a completely loopy answer.

For example, if Dave asks a question like, 'Shall we go the park?' you answer, 'Yes, but you'll have to peel it first.'

Or if Dave asks, 'What's for lunch?' you answer, 'Junction five on the M4.'

If Dave asks, 'How did you do in your maths exam?' you answer, 'A Whopper with Coke and a large fries.'

Frozen Puffs

Dave's sugar breakfast puffs will be solid
and he won't be able to get his spoon in!

You need:
Sugar puffs
A bowl
A spoon
Milk
Dave

How to do it:
Prepare Dave's favourite
cereal the night before
and put it in the freezer.

The next morning, offer Dave
his breakfast and watch him
wonder why he can't
get his spoon in!

Un-Happy Birthday

Dave won't be impressed with the smallest present he's ever received.

You need:
A big cardboard box
Wrapping paper
Sticky tape
Scissors
A piece of paper
A pen
Dave

How to do it:
Write on the piece of paper: 'Oops! I forgot to buy you anything.'

Place the piece of paper in the big box and then wrap it up like a lovely birthday present. Give Dave his massive gift and watch him grin.

Make him open it there and then, as if you can't wait for him to receive your brilliant gift! Then laugh at his grumpy face as he sees there's nothing in there apart from your note.

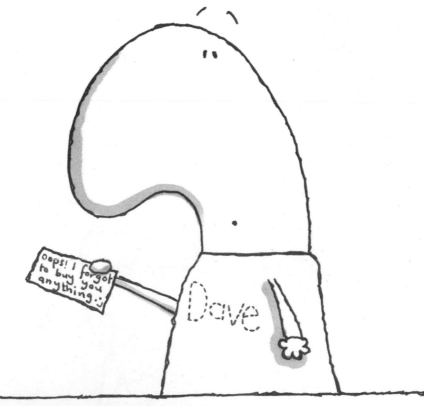

More Random Jokes

Written by Wayne Rooney's brother's milkman, who is married to a log

How do you use an ancient Egyptian doorbell?
Toot and come in.

Why did Robin Hood only rob the rich?
Because the poor didn't have anything worth stealing.

What do you get if Batman
and Robin get squashed by a
steamroller?
Flatman and Ribbon.

Why does Grandma cover
her mouth with her hand
when she sneezes?
To catch her false teeth.

What do Eskimos use to hold their
houses together?
Ig-glue.

What birds are found in Portugal?
Portu-geese.

What is the capital of France?
F.

Which fairy is the smelliest?
Stinkerbell.

Gosh!

Ooooh!

What did one octopus say to the other octopus?
'I want to hold your hand, hand, hand, hand, hand, hand, hand, hand.'

What do you get every birthday?
A year older.

How do you cure dandruff?
Cut off your head.

Waiter, do you serve fish?
Of course, sir – we'll serve anyone.

Black-Eye Telescope

Dave will get a black eye without being hit!

You need:
A cardboard tube (e.g. an empty
    kitchen roll)
Black poster paint
Paint brushes
Dave

How to do it:

Paint the whole of the inside and the outside of the tube with the black poster paint and allow it to dry. Just before you play the joke, repaint one end of the tube.

Tell Dave you have a magic telescope, and you want him to look through it at a dead pigeon you've seen in number 23's back garden.

When Dave removes the magic telescope from his face, he will have a black circle round his eye!

Don't tell him and see how long it stays there!

I see no pigeon...

THE DAILY BUM

First Edition   Monday 5th June

World - Business - Finance - Lifestyle - Travel - Sport - Weather

Woman Concealed in Man's Beard

Blah blah

Pickle Found in Vicar's Under-pants

Nick Grimshaw is Human Hanky

Blah blah

Ooooh!

Dick and Dom's **TOP FIVE** Birthday Presents

1) Bob in a box

2) A tin-foil hanky

3) No wheels

4) Tess Daly's power drill

5) Wolverhampton

Gosh!

The Long Wait

Dave will wait for hours before coming to a watery end!

You need:
A chair
A plastic cup of water
A broom
Dave

How to do it:
Stand on the chair and hold the plastic cup of water against the ceiling.

Call Dave in and ask him use the broom handle to hold the cup against the ceiling.

What?

Put the broom under this cup, quick!

Once the cup is secure between the broom handle and the ceiling, get down, pick up the chair and walk off.

Dave will be stuck there being odd (until he gets fed up and gets wet)!

Drinking Challenge

Dave won't be able to move
from the table!

You need:
Two large glasses of water
Dave

How to do it:
Make a bet
with Dave
that he can't
drink two
full glasses
of water.

Ask him to
place both
hands face
down on the
table in front
of him.

Then place a glass of water on top of each of his hands and say, 'Good luck, Dave!' and walk off.

Dave will be stuck there being odd (until he gets fed up and gets wet . . . *again*)!

Ghost at the Window

Terrify Dave with these creepy sound effects.

You need:
A drawing pin
Cotton
Dave

How to do it:
Tie the drawing pin to one end of a length of cotton, dangle it outside a window and fix it in place.

When the wind blows, the drawing pin will make the sound of some sort of ghost rattling at the window!

CLANKY
CLANKY
CLANK

Banshee Shriek

You need:
A piece of polystyrene
Dave

How to do it:
Scrape the polystyrene against a glass window to make a blood-curdling banshee shriek!

SCREECH

Whoooooooo Wail

You need:
An empty glass bottle
Dave

How to do it:
Blow across the top of
an empty bottle to make a
whooooooo wail sound.

Bad Mouse

Dave can't use his mouse (because he's stupid)!

You need:
A Post-it note
Scissors
Dave's computer mouse
Dave

How to do it:
Cut out a small rectangle from the sticky bit of the Post-it note and stick it on to the underside of Dave's computer mouse.

Watch him be flummoxed when his mouse doesn't work – bad mouse!

Wrong kind of mouse

Phantom Special Effects

You need:
A smartphone or a recordable MP3 player
Dave

How to do it:
Record sounds on a phone such as
screams, footsteps, a creaking door
or terrifying growling.

When it's dark, hide the phone and
play back the recordings!

AARGH!

WOOF!

GRRRR!

WANG!

SQUAWK

PLOP!

BLAAP!

TROT!

Dick's Wise Monkey Says . . .

Only an adult wearing
Crocs should be judged
because . . . it's WRONG!

Dave the Dummy

Dave will wonder who's in his bed?

You need:
Some spare pyjamas
Stuffing (T-shirts, socks, pants, etc.)
A dressing-up mask
Dave

How to do it:
Stuff the pyjamas with the T-shirts, socks and pants to make a body shape, and then lay it in the bed under the duvet.

Place the dressing-up mask at the top where the head should be. (You may need to make a head shape out of some balled-up T-shirts to sit the mask on!)

Hey, there's a randomer in my bed dressed as an alien!

Lower the lights and tell Dave it's bedtime. When he goes to get into bed, he'll wonder who's got there before him!

Jelly Juice

The most confusing breakfast drink!

You need:
Jelly cubes
A glass or cup
Dave

How to do it:
Follow the instructions on the
jelly packet to make the jelly
mixture (don't forget to ask for
help from a grown-up if you
need it!) and pour it into a glass
or cup.

Put the glass in the fridge overnight to set.

In the morning, offer Dave a refreshing glass of juice. Instead bring him the glass of jelly and watch his confused brain as he tries to drink the wobbly nonsense!

Answer Phoney

Confuse Dave when he is trying to talk to you on the phone.

You need:
Your phone
Dave

How to do it:
Record your own personal answerphone greeting, but instead of the usual, 'Sorry I can't answer the phone' cobblers, just say, 'Hello?' then pause for ages and say, 'Hello? *Hello?*' Now stop recording.

Wait for Dave to call you and let it ring to answerphone. He won't know what's going on and you'll *love* listening to his confused messages.

131

Monster Jokes

Written by Crumplehorn von Dimblehump, the very angry, dribbly, granny-eating, bat-winged, one-legged, lolly-licking monster from Boo-Boo Swamp

How do you make a witch itch?
Take away her 'w'.

What would you say if you met a monster with three heads?
'Hello, hello, hello!'

What will a monster eat in a restaurant?
The waiter.

What do you call a nervous witch?
A 'twitch'.

What is a sea monster's favourite dish?
Fish and ships.

Why does the ghost keep coming back to the library for more books?
Because it goes through them so quickly.

Wakey Wakey!

Give Dave a rude awakening at 3.00 a.m.

You need:
All the alarm clocks and
 mobile phones in your house
Dave

How to do it:
When Dave has gone to bed, collect every alarm clock and mobile phone in the house and set the alarms for 3.00 a.m., then place them in Dave's room.

Then just wait and enjoy Dave's confused screams when he's woken up at 3.00 a.m.

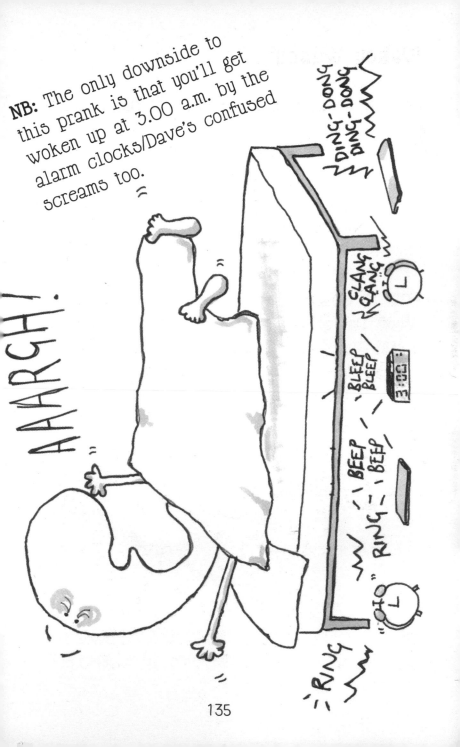

Blanky, Blanky, Blanky!

Fill in the blanks to make up your own stories.

Mr Grumbly the teddy bear woke up one

morning and shouted, '_____!' The

reason he shouted it was because there was

_____ all over his walls. In the

middle of the night a _____ had

crept in and thrown the _____

everywhere. Unknown to Mr Grumbly, it was

also all over his face.

He went to the bathroom, looked in the mirror

and this time shouted, '_____!'

He then decided to change his name to Mrs

_____. Silly old Mr Grumbly!

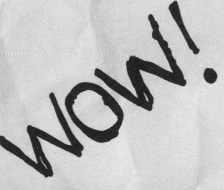

Heavy Bag

When Dave goes to school, he won't be able to work out why his bag is so flippin' heavy!

You need:
Some bottles of water
Dave's bag
Dave

How to do it:
When Dave is in a different room, sneak the bottles of water into his school bag or rucksack and make sure they're hidden under all his books.

Water Flavour
Water!

with Added Water

PLUS 10% FREE WATER

Contains water.

When Dave picks up his bag to go to school, he'll think he's become a weakling overnight!

THE DAILY BUM

First Edition   Monday 5th June

World - Business - Finance - Lifestyle - Travel - Sport - Weather

Japan to Be Moved to Just Outside Wales

Blah blah blah blah blah blah blah blah blah blah blah blah blah blah blah blah blah blah blah blah blah blah blah blah blah blah blah blah blah blah blah blah blah blah blah blah blah blah blah blah blah blah blah blah blah blah blah blah blah blah blah blah blah blah blah blah blah blah blah blah blah blah blah blah blah blah blah blah blah blah blah blah

Joy Over Hamster-and-Apple-Flavour Crisps

Motorway Service Stations to Be Replaced by Elton John Health Spas

Blah blah

Crazy, Crazy Kitchen Cupboards

Dave can't work out why the tins are in the glasses cupboard and the cereal is in the pan cupboard!

You need:
A kitchen
Dave

Cupboard Art

How to do it:
When Dave is out, simply take *everything* out of the kitchen cupboards and put the contents back into other cupboards in the kitchen.

When Dave comes back, ask him to make you a cup of tea. His brain will fry!

Bog Bubbles

Make Dave's toilet extra frothy!

You need:
A toilet
Washing-up liquid
Dave

How to do it:
Pour some washing-up liquid into the toilet, then when Dave goes pee pee, his toilet goes bubbly!

Gosh!

Minty Biccy

Dave's favourite biscuits will clean his teeth whilst he's eating them!

You need:
Biscuits with a cream filling
Toothpaste
Dave

How to do it:
Scrape out the cream of a biscuit and re-fill it with toothpaste. Put the halves of the biscuit back together and on to a plate.

Offer Dave his favourite biccy-wiccy and watch him wonder why his biscuit is minty!

Beach Bum

While on a beach holiday, watch Dave's bum
fly down a hole!

You need:
A towel
A spade
Dave

How to do it:

When Dave goes for a dip in the sea, dig a
hole under his towel and put the towel back
over it.

When Dave gets back and lies down,
his bum will fall into the hole!

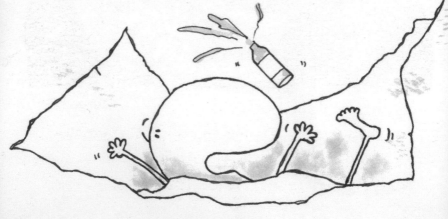

Foam Face

Watch Dave pie himself in the face while asleep.

You need:
Shaving foam
Dave (asleep)

How to do it:
While Dave is sleeping, secretly squirt some shaving foam into the palms of his hands.

Lightly tickle Dave's nose and when he reaches up to itch his schnozz he will get a face full of foam pie!

The Incredible Shrinking Clothes

Dave will think he's suddenly grown
(or his clothes have shrunk)!

You need:
Dave's school uniform but
   in smaller sizes
Dave

How to do it:
While Dave is
lazing about in
bed, replace his
school uniform
with the smaller
version.

When he goes to
get dressed, none of
it will fit and he'll
think he's turned into
a giant overnight!

Dick's Wise Monkey Says . . .

When you dip your
toes into the puddle
of youth, make sure it's
not a puddle of piddle.

String of Pants

When Dave goes to get his undercrackers out of his drawers, he finds they're all joined together!

You need:
Needle
Cotton
Dave's pants
Dave

How to do it:
While Dave is out, use the needle and thread to stitch the edge of one pair of Dave's pants to the edge of the next pair.

When you have a long string of pants, put them back in Dave's chest of drawers, laying one on top of another (like a zigzag) so they just look like an ordinary pile of pants.

When Dave goes to get some clean pants in the morning, laugh at his confused face as he keeps on pulling out pair after pair after pair.

THE DAILY BUM

First Edition   Monday 5th June

World - Business - Finance - Lifestyle - Travel - Sport - Weather

Fishcake Contains Mersey-bum Fish

Blah blah blah blah blah blah blah blah blah blah blah blah blah blah blah blah blah blah blah blah blah blah blah blah blah blah blah blah blah blah blah blah blah blah blah blah blah blah blah blah blah blah blah blah blah blah blah blah blah blah blah blah blah blah blah blah blah blah blah blah blah blah blah blah blah blah blah blah blah blah blah blah blah blah blah blah blah blah blah blah blah blah blah blah blah blah blah blah blah blah blah blah blah blah blah blah blah blah blah blah Blah blah blah blah blah blah blah blah blah blah blah blah blah blah blah blah blah blah blah blah blah blah blah blah blah blah blah blah blah blah blah blah blah blah blah blah

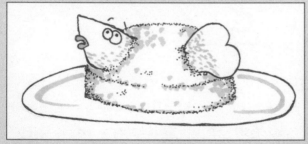

See-through Windows Made Illegal in Norwich

Alan Titchmarsh Pregnant

Blah blah blah blah blah blah blah blah blah blah blah blah blah blah blah blah blah blah blah blah blah blah blah blah blah blah blah blah blah blah blah blah blah blah blah blah blah blah blah blah blah blah blah blah blah blah blah blah blah blah blah blah blah blah blah blah blah blah blah blah blah blah blah blah blah blah blah blah blah blah blah blah blah blah blah blah blah blah blah blah blah blah blah blah blah blah blah blah Blah blah blah blah blah blah blah blah blah blah blah blah blah blah blah blah blah blah blah blah blah blah blah blah blah blah blah blah blah blah blah blah blah blah blah blah blah blah blah blah blah blah blah blah blah blah blah blah blah blah blah blah blah blah blah blah blah blah blah blah blah blah blah blah blah blah blah blah blah blah blah blah blah blah blah blah blah blah blah blah blah blah blah blah

Ooooh

Balloony

Dave's bedroom will be rammed to the rafters with balloons.

You need:
Lots of balloons
Dave's bedroom
Dave

How to do it:
With the help of an adult, blow up as many balloons as you can and fill Dave's bedroom up so he can only just get in.

When Dave comes home, ask him to get something from his room and when he opens the door he'll see only balloons.

Wallpaper Switchy-Swatch

Dave will become a super-fan overnight!

You need:
A big picture of Prince Charles's* face
A photocopier
Blu-tack
Dave's bedroom
Dave

How to do it:
At the library, photocopy the picture
of Prince Charles a hundred times.

While Dave is out, use the
Blu-tack to stick the pictures
all over his bedroom.

When Dave comes home and goes
into his room, follow him, laugh
and do a bad impression of Prince
Charles over and over again!

*Or Stephen Mulhern's face, your mum's face,
or your face . . . anyone's face, really.

Don't Be Late!

Dave will be an hour early for everything.

You need:
All the clocks, phones and computers
   (anything showing the time) in
   your house
Dave

How to do it:
While Dave is distracted by watching TV,
reset all the clocks in the house to an hour
later.

Sit back and watch as
Dave realizes the time,
rushes around and
leaves the house in a
hurry, only to arrive
an hour too early!

Cereal Mix-Up

Dave hates choco pops with a passion!

You need:
All the cereal in your house
Dave

How to do it:
The night
before you
want to prank
Dave, take all
the plastic
cereal bags out
of the cereal
boxes and
put them into
different boxes.

Dave will be
furious when he
pours himself some
cornflakes only to
discover he's got
choco pops instead!

Cereal Nuts

Dave hates nuts with a passion! (He's just a nut hater. He's **not** allergic to nuts. **DO NOT** play this prank on anyone with a nut allergy!)

You need:
Dave's favourite cereal
A bag of nuts and seeds
A container
Dave

How to do it:
Pour Dave's favourite cereal into another container, then refill the plastic cereal bag with nuts and seeds.

When Dave goes to have his brekkie and pours himself a bowl of nuts, he'll be even more furious than that time he thought he was having cornflakes but got choco pops instead!

Dick and Dom's **TOP FIVE** Best Ways to Pass Time on a Long Car Journey

1) Use your dad's head as a bongo

2) For the whole journey ask your mum when she is going to grow a beard

3) Dress up as Steve Backshall and do the fandango

4) Shave a monkey

5) Play I spy with your eyes closed

ahHEADLINES FROM

THE DAILY BUM

First Edition   Monday 5th June

World - Business - Finance - Lifestyle - Travel - Sport - Weather

Water to Be Made Illegal

Blah blah blah blah blah blah blah blah blah blah blah blah blah blah blah blah blah blah blah blah blah blah blah blah blah blah blah blah blah blah blah blah blah blah blah blah blah blah blah blah blah blah blah blah blah blah blah blah blah blah blah blah blah blah blah blah blah blah blah blah blah blah blah blah blah blah blah blah blah blah blah blah blah blah blah blah blah blah blah blah Blah blah blah blah blah blah blah blah blah blah blah blah blah blah blah blah blah blah blah blah blah blah blah blah blah blah blah blah blah blah blah blah blah blah blah blah blah blah blah blah blah blah blah blah blah blah blah blah blah blah blah blah blah blah blah blah blah blah blah blah blah blah blah blah blah blah blah blah blah blah blah blah blah blah blah blah blah blah

The Hairy Bikers Found in Giraffe's Neck

Swimming in Fat Is 'One of Your Five a Day' Say Doctors

Blah blah

Ooooh!

Konnichiwa

Dave doesn't know Japanese!

You need:
Dave's phone
Dave

How to do it:
Secretly change the language setting
in Dave's phone to Japanese.

Dave doesn't know Japanese, so it
will take ages for him to work out
how to turn it back!

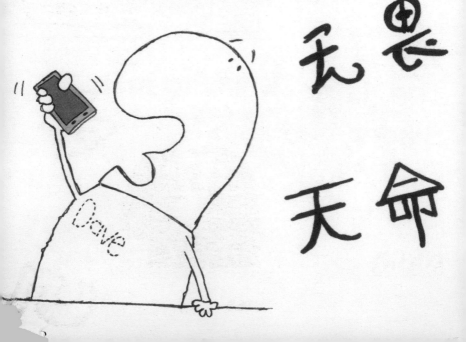

Dick and Dom's **TOP FIVE**
Things to Wear Instead of a Hat

1) A colander full of cabbage

2) Andy Murray's mum

3) Some bits

4) A petrol-powered pollack

JUST CHECK THAT OUT! AN AMAZING OUTFIT, AND A PETROL-POWERED POLLACK. THAT IS A GREAT LOOK.

5) A frat

Din-Din Mix-Up

Dave won't know what to eat with!

You need:
Kitchen utensils such as ladles,
   whisks and serving spoons
Saucers
Dave

How to do it:
When you get asked
to lay the table, use
saucers instead of
dinner plates, and
kitchen utensils
instead of cutlery.

Make sure anyone else having
dinner with you (apart from
Dave) is in on the joke and acts
as if your choice of plates and
cutlery is completely normal.

Serve Dave his tiny
dinner and watch him
try to work out how
to eat it with a
rolling pin!

Dave

Face Plant

Dave will walk around all day with a picture of your face attached to his back!

You need:
A print-out of your face
Scissors
Sticky tape
Dave

Er...

How to do it:
Print out a picture of your face and cut it out using the scissors.

When you next see Dave, give him a really friendly pat on the back. At the same time, use some sticky tape to stick your face to Dave's back.

WHAT?

Sit back and see how long it takes for him to notice!

Homemade Itching Powder

Dave will be itchy, but he won't know why!

You need:
Some of your hair (collect it the
   next time you have your hair cut)
Scissors
Dave

How to do it:
Cut up the hair you have
collected into tiny pieces and
keep it in a little pot or plastic
bag in your pocket.

Next time you see Dave, pretend
to tuck in the label on the back
of his jumper. At the same time,
take a pinch of hair from the
stash in your pocket and sprinkle
it down Dave's back.

Then simply
wait and watch
him itch!

AAARGH!

Dave

THE DAILY BUM

First Edition   Monday 5th June

World - Business - Finance - Lifestyle - Travel - Sport - Weather

Father's 150mph Sneeze
Blows Mother's Hair Off

Blah blah blah blah blah
blah blah blah blah blah
blah blah blah blah blah
blah blah blah blah blah
blah blah blah blah blah
blah blah blah blah blah
blah blah blah blah blah
blah blah blah blah blah
blah blah blah blah blah
blah blah blah blah blah
blah blah blah blah blah
blah blah blah blah blah
blah blah blah blah blah
blah blah blah blah blah
blah blah blah blah blah
blah blah blah blah blah
blah blah blah blah blah
blah blah blah blah blah
blah blah blah blah blah blah

Hospitals Resort to Hiring Bouncy Castles to Save Lives

Pigs' Milk Given to the Royal Air Force

Blah blah blah blah blah blah blah blah blah blah blah blah blah
blah blah blah blah blah blah blah blah blah blah blah blah blah
blah blah blah blah blah blah blah blah blah blah blah blah blah
blah blah blah blah blah blah blah blah blah blah blah blah blah
blah blah blah blah blah blah blah blah blah blah blah blah blah
blah blah blah blah blah blah blah blah blah blah blah blah blah
blah blah blah blah blah blah blah blah blah blah blah blah blah
blah blah blah blah blah blah blah blah blah blah blah blah blah
blah blah blah blah blah blah blah blah blah blah blah blah blah
blah blah blah blah blah blah blah blah blah blah blah blah blah

170

Ooooh!

Dick's Wise Monkey Says . . .

Do not let the
behaviour of others
destroy your inner piece . . .
of carrot cake!

Blanky, Blanky, Blanky!

Fill in the blanks to make up your own stories.

Gosh!

A man from Liverpool went to the

river to catch a Mersey-bum fish

using a _____. Instead of

catching a Mersey-bum fish, he caught a

_____.

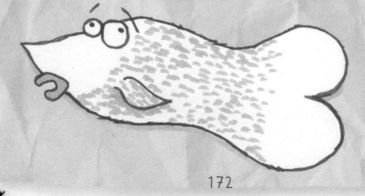

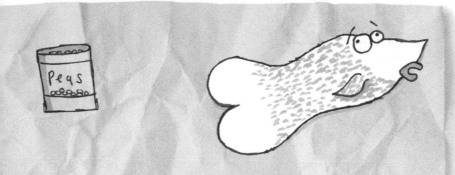

He didn't like the look of it, so he put it

back and then caught a _____

instead. Finally a Mersey-bum fish popped

his head out of the water and said, '_____

_____!'

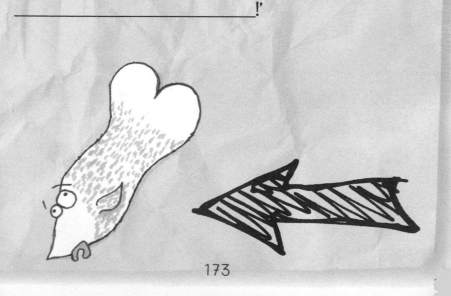

Banana-Rama

Dave's banana will fall to bits.

You need:
A needle
A banana
Dave

How to do it:
Push the
needle into
the banana
and move
it from side
to side so
the tip of the
needle makes
contact with the
inside of the skin on the
other side of the banana.

174

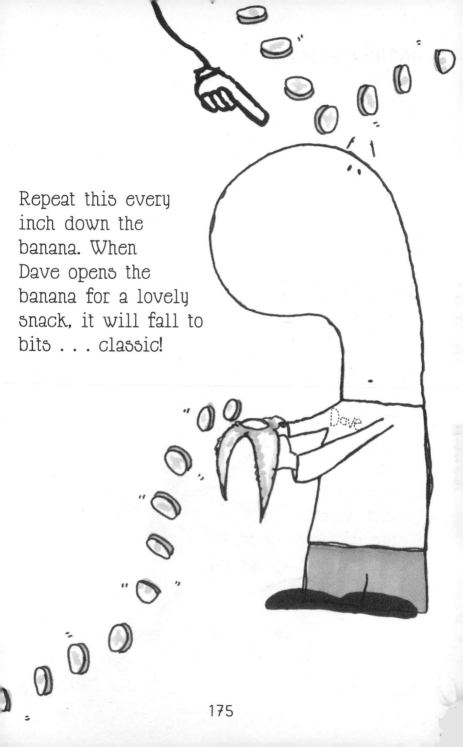

Repeat this every inch down the banana. When Dave opens the banana for a lovely snack, it will fall to bits . . . classic!

Dave

DIY Fake Doggy Doo

Dave will think the dog's done a doo on the carpet!

> ***You need:***
> Brown poster paint
> Modelling clay
> Dave

How to do it:
In secret, create a convincing dog-poo shape out of modelling clay. Let it dry and go hard – then paint it brown and let the paint dry too.

Next, place the clay poo on the floor and scream out, 'Dave, the doggy's done bad things on the carpet!'

DOGGY'S DONE BAD THINGS. AAAARGH!

Dave will run in, squirm and say, 'But we haven't got a dog . . . ?'

THE DAILY BUM

First Edition   Monday 5th June

World - Business - Finance - Lifestyle - Travel - Sport - Weather

Locals Throw Teacups at Flying Saucers

blah blah blah blah blah blah blah blah
blah blah blah blah blah blah blah blah
blah blah blah blah blah blah blah blah
blah blah blah blah blah blah blah blah
blah blah blah blah blah blah blah blah
blah blah blah blah blah blah blah blah
blah blah blah blah blah blah blah blah
blah blah blah blah blah blah blah blah
blah blah blah blah blah blah blah blah
blah blah blah blah blah blah blah blah
blah blah blah blah blah blah blah blah
blah blah blah blah blah blah blah blah
blah blah blah blah blah blah blah blah
blah blah blah blah blah blah blah blah
blah blah blah blah blah blah blah blah
blah blah blah blah blah blah blah blah
blah blah blah blah blah blah blah blah
blah blah blah blah blah blah blah blah
blah blah blah blah blah blah blah blah

Willy Wonka 'Allergic' to Chocolate

Man Swallows Jupiter

blah blah blah blah blah blah blah blah blah blah blah blah blah blah
blah blah blah blah blah blah blah blah blah blah blah blah blah blah
blah blah blah blah blah blah blah blah blah blah blah blah blah blah
blah blah blah blah blah blah blah blah blah blah blah blah blah blah
blah blah blah blah blah blah blah blah blah blah blah blah blah blah
blah blah blah blah blah blah blah blah blah blah blah blah blah blah
blah blah blah blah blah blah blah blah blah blah blah blah blah blah
blah blah blah blah blah blah blah blah blah blah blah blah blah blah
blah blah blah blah blah blah blah blah blah blah blah blah blah blah
blah blah blah blah blah blah blah blah blah blah blah blah blah blah
blah blah blah blah blah blah blah blah blah blah blah blah blah blah

178

Ooooh!

Animal Jokes

Written by five hamsters named Ping, Plop, Pang, Pow and Pooh, jumping up and down on a 1970s typewriter

What should you do if a dog eats your pencil?
Use a pen instead.

What was on special offer at the pet shop?
'Buy one dog, get one flea.'

What kind of gum do bees chew?
Bumble gum.

NEW NECTAR FLAVOUR
Bumble Gum

What do you get if you cross a skunk
with a bat?
A nasty smell that hangs around all day.

What sound do hedgehogs
make when they kiss?
'Ouch!'

What goes 'OOOOO!'?
A cow with no lips.

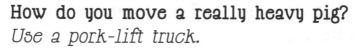

How do you move a really heavy pig?
Use a pork-lift truck.

What do you call someone with an elephant on his head?
Squashed.

Why do penguins carry fish in their beaks?
Because they don't have any pockets.

What do you call a rabbit with
no clothes on?
A bare hare.

What did the
hedgehog say
to the cactus?
*'Is that you,
Mummy?'*

Why do giraffes have such long necks?
Because they've got really stinky feet.

Snot Head

Dave will get it on the back of his head!

You need:
An egg cup of water
Dave

How to do it:
Hide the egg cup of water in your hand.
Creep up behind Dave, pretend to sneeze,
then throw the water over the
back of Dave's
head.

Toffee Onion

Dave will get a stinky surprise when he bites into this toffee treat!

You need:
An onion about the size of an apple
An adult
A lollipop stick
Sugar, golden syrup and butter
Dave

How to do it:
Ask an adult to make you some toffee-apple sauce using the sugar, golden syrup and butter.

Peel the onion, put it on the lollipop stick and ask your adult to coat it in the sticky toffee sauce. Let it set and cool.

When Dave
comes home from
school, offer
him a nice, juicy
'toffee apple'
and watch his
silly face when
he bites into
a toffee onion
instead!

Doughnut Surprise

Dave will never trust you again once he's tried this unexpectedly mayonnaisy snack.

You need:
A doughnut with no filling
Mayonnaise
An icing bag with a plastic nozzle
Dave

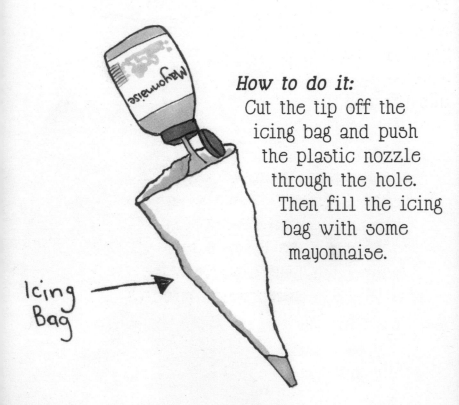

How to do it:
Cut the tip off the icing bag and push the plastic nozzle through the hole. Then fill the icing bag with some mayonnaise.

Icing Bag

Doughnut

Take the doughnut
with no filling and,
using the icing bag,
squeeze the mayo
into the middle.

Offer Dave the
delicious doughnut
and laugh at his
silly face when
he takes a bite
and discovers the
mayonnaise middle!

Happy Cleaning

Dave doesn't want to make a watery mess . . . but he'll have to!

Oooh!

You need:
A glass
Water
Postcard
Pen
Dave

How to do it:
Fill a glass
to the top
with water
and place the
postcard on top.

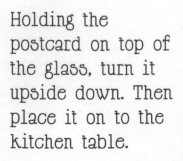

Holding the postcard on top of the glass, turn it upside down. Then place it on to the kitchen table.

Keeping pressure on the glass by pushing it down with one hand, remove the postcard.

You will now have an upside down glass full of water on the table.

WOW!

Gosh!

Write on the postcard, 'HAPPY CLEANING, DAVE!' ... then leg it!

Do As You're Told!

Dave won't know where to look.

You need:
Paper
Pen
Blu-tack
Floor and ceiling
Dave

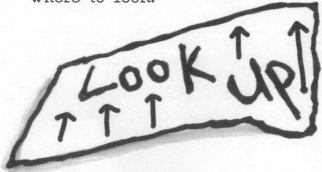

How to do it:

Write on one sheet of paper 'look up' and on another 'look down'. Blu-tack 'look up' to the floor and 'look down' to the ceiling.

Ask Dave to read your notices and watch him not knowing where to look.

Even More Random Jokes

Written by a fish who is now dead because he had to write the jokes out of water so that the paper didn't get soggy

What's the coldest city in Germany?
Brrr-lin!

Which language is always in a hurry?
Russian! Russian here . . . Russian there.

Do you turn your computer on with your left hand or your right hand?
Neither, I use the on/off switch.

What did Hamlet say when he was thinking of sending a message?
To e or not to e, that is the question.

How did the Vikings send secret messages?
In Norse code.

Which country is always starving?
Hungary!

Who invented the fireplace?
Alfred the Grate.

Why were the early days of history called the Dark Ages?
Because they were full of knights.

What was King Arthur's favourite game?
Knights and crosses.

Why do squirrels sneak
into the library to use the
computers?
To go on the inter-nut!

How did the school cook make
an apple crumble?
She hit it with a frying pan.

What's the most slippery country
in the world?
Greece!

Dick's Wise Monkey Says . . .
Happiness does not
come from within you, or
from others, or from possessions.
Happiness comes from ginger nuts.

Stuck!

Dave won't be able to read.

You need:
A copy of Dave's favourite book
(get one from a charity shop –
don't use Dave's actual copy!)
A glue stick
Dave

How to do it:
This will take *some**
time . . . All you
have to do is stick
every page of Dave's
book together then,
when it's dry, leave
it on Dave's bed.

*Ages and ages.

When Dave comes to open up
his book for a spot of bedtime
reading and realizes he can't,
he'll think he's gone loopy!

Squashed Fly

Dave won't believe his eyes when you eat a dead fly!

> *You need:*
> A raisin
> Dave

How to do it:
While talking to Dave about the price of chips, pretend to follow a fly around the room with your eyes. Then suddenly clap your hands together as if you've squashed it!

Quickly show Dave the thing you've squashed in your hand. Then proceed to eat the dead fly.

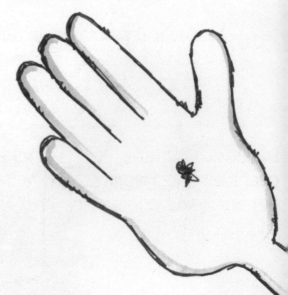

Floating Lump

Dave's tea won't be sweet, just floaty!

You need:
Some polystyrene
A mug of tea
Dave

How to do it:
In secret, break off some pieces of polystyrene and make them look the same shape as lumps of sugar, then pop them on top of the sugar bowl.

Make Dave a cup of tea and ask if he wants sugar. When he says 'yes', drop in a few lumps of your 'special' sugar.

Laugh at Dave's confused face when the sugar just floats and doesn't sink.

Dick and Dom's **TOP FIVE** Board Games

1) Lads and Ladders

2) Hungry, Hungry Hippies

3) Connect 1

4) Unsuccessful Operation

5) Guess Who . . . Dropped Their Guts?

Clean Your Glasses

Dave will be gobsmacked when you do magic with your specs.

You need:
A pair of old spectacles
A small cloth or handkerchief
Dave

How to do it:
Before you meet Dave, get an adult to carefully remove the lenses from the glasses frames.

When you meet Dave, wear the glasses. Take out the handkerchief and act as though you're going to clean your specs. Then suddenly pull the hanky through the frames!

Dave will be dead impressed and think you've done glasses magic.

Lumpy Tummy

Dave will think you have an alien in your belly!

You need:
A jumper
Dave

How to do it:
Wearing the jumper, put the end of one sleeve completely over your other hand and sleeve.

With the jumper still on, slide your arm out of the sleeve and in front of your tummy. It will look like you are holding your hands together in front of you.

AARGH ALIEN

When Dave comes up to say hello, freak him out by moving your hidden hand around like an alien in your tummy!

HEADLINES FROM

THE DAILY BUM

First Edition   Monday 5th June

World - Business - Finance - Lifestyle - Travel - Sport - Weather

Angry Banjo to Be Put Down

Blah blah

Eel Found in Man Bag

Police to Arrest Everyone by 21 February

Blah blah blah blah blah blah blah blah blah blah blah blah blah blah blah blah blah blah blah blah blah blah blah blah blah blah blah blah blah blah blah blah blah blah blah

Claudia Winkleman to Star in *Rocky* Remake

Blah blah

Oooo!

Plop on the Seat

Dave will wonder who's plopped on the toilet seat.

You need:
A toilet-roll tube
Dave

How to do it:
Rip up the bog-roll tube into long strips then soak them with water from the sink.

When the strips have gone all soggy, mould them into the shape of a plop and leave it on the seat as a treat for Dave to find, then walk out.

Banana-Skin Surprise

A twist on a classic!

You need:
A very soft banana
Dave

How to do it:
Take the soft banana out of its skin,
place the skin on the ground and hide
the soft banana behind your back.

When Dave walks into the room,
point at the banana skin and
say, 'Watch your step, Dave!'
When he looks down, throw the
banana at him!

NB: Only do this in rooms with hard floors –
unless you want to spend the next million
years scrubbing banana out of the carpet!

Clown Time!

Make Dave cack himself when he wakes up and sees a clown.

You need:
Face paints
A colourful wig*
A red nose*
Dave

*Optional.

How to do it:
When Dave is asleep, use the face paints (and wig and red nose if you have them) to make yourself look like a very scary clown. To wake up Dave, put your face right next to his and shout, 'CLOWN TIME!'

Blanky, Blanky, Blanky!

Fill in the blanks to make up your own stories.

The Queen went to _____

and decided to mow the lawn. Instead

of using a lawnmower, however, she

used a _____. Prince Charles

appeared and said, '_____,

_____!'

Ooooh!

Oh dear, Her Majesty thought. I'd better go

to the shops and buy a _____!

She then used this to finish off the lawn.

Once she had finished she declared to

the nation that she was _____

and _____, and would

_____ immediately.

Dick and Dom's Big Fat Crossword

Across:

1. An alternative word for donkey (3)
7. Another word for toilet roll* (5, 5)
8. The one lesson at school you really don't want to forget your stuff for (2)
10. My face when you are talking to me (5)
11. The Queen loves this meaty treat (4)
12. Country where stinky-cheese eaters live (6)

Down:

2. Another name for an MP (6)
3. The resulting injury of a knee slide, elbow scrape or wall scratch* (6, 4)
4. A dusty sweet from your nan's handbag* (5)
5. Sometimes found in teacups (5)
6. My dog loves to chew on this (6)
8. On your birthday, your umbutu* will send you money in the _ _ _ _ (4)
9. The singular of pants (4)

*See *Dick and Dom's Slightly Naughty but Very Silly Words*. Or cheat and look at the answers.

See page 232 for answers

Music Jokes

Written by Arthur Sneezeman, the ten-ton trombonist from Trumpton who plays the trombone with his feet

What do you get when
you drop a piano down a
mineshaft?
A flat minor.

What do you get when
you drop a piano on an
army base?
A flat major.

What musical key do
cows sing in?
Beef flat.

What type of music are
balloons scared of?
Pop music!

What makes
pirates such good
singers?
*They can hit the
high Cs!*

Why are musicians so
rubbish at maths?
*Because they only
learn to count to four!
One, two . . . a-one,
two, three, four!*

Spider Hider

Dave hates spiders . . . so Dave will really hate this one!

You need:
A large plastic spider
Some string or elastic
Dave

How to do it:
After Dave has gone to bed, tie the plastic spider to the string, then hang it level with where Dave's face would be outside his bedroom door.

When Dave walks out of his room in the morning . . . you'll hear the screams!

AAARGH!

Dave

Jelly Worms

Dave will think you've lost the plot
when you start eating worms.

You need:
A cup
Drinking straws
Jelly cubes
Dave

How to do it:
Pack all the straws into the cup so they are
standing up straight. Get an adult to make the
jelly mixture and pour it down all the straws
and into the cup, until the mixture is up
to the top of the straws. Then put it in the
fridge to set.

Once the jelly is set, pour warm
water on to the straws and the jelly
worm shapes will come sliding out.

Hide a jelly worm in your hand and tell Dave
to come into the garden. Now reach behind a
bush, show Dave the jelly worm . . . and eat it!

Lotto Win-Win!

Dave will think you've both
won millions, but you haven't.

> ### You need:
> An adult
> Last week's paper with the Lotto
>   results in it
> Dave

How to do it:

Write down the winning Lotto numbers from
last week's paper. Then get your grown-up to
go to the shop and buy a Lotto ticket with
exactly the same numbers on it.

Leave last week's paper and the new Lotto
ticket on the kitchen table and ask Dave
to check the numbers.

He'll dance, he'll sing and
then, when he realizes
the paper is out of
date . . . he'll cry!

Nooo

Dick's Wise Monkey Says . . .

When all else fails and
the forces of the world seem
against you . . . climb inside your
own mouth and read *The Hobbit*.

217

Supersize Shop

Dave won't believe how much shopping he has!

You need:
A shop
Dave

How to do it:
Surprise the grown-ups you live with by saying that you and Dave will do the weekly shop, but make sure you put Dave in charge of the shopping list *and* the money.

While helping Dave do the shopping, when he's not looking, keep adding more and more rubbish things to the trolley.

When you get to the till, Dave will be totally confused!

Tic-Tac Teeth

Time for the
dentist as all
your teeth fall
out!

You need:
White Tic Tacs
Dave

How to do it:
Tell Dave you need to
go to the dentist. When
you get there, secretly
fill your mouth with white
Tic-Tac sweets.

While Dave is talking to
the receptionist, surprise them both
by letting the Tic Tacs slowly fall
out of your mouth and into your hand.
Now curl your lips into your mouth.

Teeth . . . gone!

HEADLINES FROM

THE DAILY BUM

First Edition   Monday 5th June

World - Business - Finance - Lifestyle - Travel - Sport - Weather

Cycling Dinosaur Disrupts Builders

Blah blah blah blah blah blah blah blah
blah blah blah blah blah blah blah blah
blah blah blah blah blah blah blah blah
blah blah blah blah blah blah blah blah
blah blah blah blah blah blah blah blah
blah blah blah blah blah blah blah blah
blah blah blah blah blah blah blah blah
blah blah blah blah blah blah blah blah

Dog Has Tongue the Size of Car

Blah blah blah blah blah blah blah
blah blah blah blah blah blah blah
blah blah blah blah blah blah blah
blah blah blah blah blah blah blah
blah blah blah blah blah blah blah
blah blah blah blah blah blah blah

Obama Biography Title Leaked: Obama Llama Ding Dong

Blah blah blah blah blah blah blah blah blah blah blah blah blah
blah blah blah blah blah blah blah blah blah blah blah blah blah
blah blah blah blah blah blah blah blah blah blah blah blah blah
blah blah blah blah blah blah blah blah blah blah blah blah blah
blah blah blah blah blah blah blah blah blah blah blah blah blah
blah blah blah blah blah blah blah blah blah blah blah blah blah
blah blah blah blah blah blah blah blah blah blah blah blah blah
blah blah blah blah blah blah blah blah blah blah blah blah blah

221

Ooooh!

Big-Car Surprise

This is a joke that can only be played on grown-ups, so make sure you pick someone who'll find this funny!

You need:
A grown-up with a car (or Dave)

How to do it:
While the driver of the car is out paying for the petrol, in the shop or bank, turn everything on or up: windscreen wipers, stereo volume, fan heaters, headlights.

When they return to the car and turn the ignition on . . . it's party time!

Football Jokes

Written by Billy Bongos — an eighty-six-year-old retired, two-headed football referee from Wrexham

Doctor, Doctor. I feel like a referee! *DOCTOR: So do I — let's go and buy a couple at the corner shop.*

DOM: Dick, do you have holes in your football shorts? *DICK: No.* DOM: Then how do you get them on?

When is a footballer like a baby? *When it dribbles.*

What was that film about
referees called?
The Umpire Strikes Back.

What can light up a dull
evening?
A football match.

Why did the referee have a
sausage stuck behind his ear?
*Because he's eaten his whistle
at lunchtime!*

Why can't a car play football?
Because it's only got one boot.

DICK: What kind of leather makes the best football boots?
DOM: I don't know. But banana peel makes the best slippers!

Why was the mummy no good at football?
Because he was too wrapped up in himself.

Doctor! Come quickly! The referee has swallowed his biro! What can we do?
DOCTOR: *Use another one until I get there.*

Dick and Dom were at the
football discussing their
packed lunches.
DICK: What have you got?
DOM: Tongue sandwiches.
*DICK: That's disgusting. I
couldn't eat something that had
come out of an animal's mouth.*
DOM: What have you got?
DICK: Egg sandwiches.

**DOM'S UNCLE: I'll teach
you to kick footballs at my
greenhouse!**
*DOM: I wish you would –
I keep missing.*

Special Delivery

Dave will be excited by his mystery
package – until he opens it.

You need:
A cardboard box big enough to hide in
Dave

How to do it:
Go to Dave's house, ring the
bell and then hide in the
box. When he tries to
open it . . . yell
'SURPRISE!', jump
out and scare
the hell out
of him.

Real 'Sponge' Cake

It looks delicious. It tastes . . . spongy.

Sponge

You need:
A bath sponge
Scissors
Chocolate cream
Cake decorations (hundreds
    and thousands, silver balls, etc.)
Dave

How to do it:
Use the scissors to cut the bath sponge into
three sections, nice and neatly, so they look
like cake slices. Decorate the slices with
chocolate cream and cover them all over
with cake decorations.

When Dave comes in, offer him a
nice slice of 'sponge' cake. Take a
slice yourself but put off eating it.

'Sponge' Cake

When Dave takes a bite,
he's in for a spongy surprise!

Dick and Dom's **TOP FIVE**
Sandwich Fillings

1) Tongue and pickle

2) Monkey mouth and Marmite

3) Harry Hill and ham

4) Bieber and beetroot

5) Eggy-egg

Fakey Flies

Dave will think the house has been infested!

You need:
Some fake flies
   (can be bought
   in a fancy-
   dress or joke
   shop)
Dave

How to do it:
Place the fake
flies everywhere
around the house
– in Dave's
shoes, in his
ice cubes, in the
sugar bowl and
in his bed!

YAY!

Catching Nothing

Dave will think you're a magician!

You need:
A brown paper bag
Dave

How to do it:
Hold the paper bag with your thumb
on the outside and your middle
finger opposite it on the inside.

With your other hand pretend to grab a
ball, throw it into the air and watch it
land in the bag. At this point click your
fingers together and the bag will sound
and look like something has landed in it!

Answers

Page 96
Dick and
Dom's
Slightly-
Naughty-but-
Very-Silly
Wordsearch

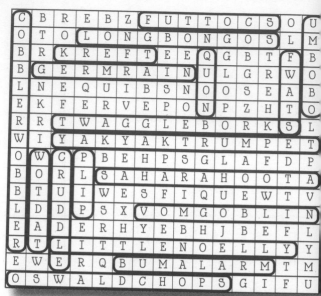

Page 210
Dick and
Dom's
Big Fat
Crossword